My Baby Big Sister

Cathy Blanford

ISBN 13:9781451579765
ISBN 10:1451579764
Library of Congress Control Number: 2010905482

MY BABY BIG SISTER
www.MyBabyBigSister.com

Designed by Ellie Searl

Ananda Press
Western Springs, IL
Printed in USA

Proceeds from MY BABY BIG SISTER will support the work of Still Missed, a perinatal loss support program located in Hinsdale, Illinois. Still Missed, which is a program of the Adventist Midwest Health Systems, has been in existence since 1987. For further information regarding Still Missed or perinatal loss and grief, call 630 856-4497 or e-mail stillmissed@ahss.org.

With gratitude to the Paus family
who contributed to this book
in loving memory of their son and brother, Eliot.

A MESSAGE TO PARENTS

I've written this book for all of you who are raising a child who was born after you had a baby die. This child has come into a family that has experienced a very important life event. While the subsequent child did not actually experience the loss of his sibling and may not be personally grieving for this baby who died, he is now a member of a family in which the loss of a baby is a significant piece of the family story.

The most important thing for your subsequent child is to be wholeheartedly welcomed into the family and to be totally wanted and loved for who he is himself. However, because your baby is a part of your family's story, your subsequent child will need help understanding who this person was and what significance your baby had in the family.

While this may not be a personal loss for your child, he may still experience curiosity and some feelings of missing what might have been. There is a difference between your reality of the baby and your child's experience. For instance, it would be a normal reaction for your child to be less interested, to sometimes be tired of the sadness, and to want to have the parents' attention focused on him instead of on memories of the baby.

While this story has specific details that may not be relevant to your situation, the intention is to produce a universal story, one to which your child will be able to relate. Most pages have a box with words in it especially for you to help you understand why the particular text was chosen and how best you can help your child. You may want to read the book through first before reading it with your child.

Perhaps the most important thing that you can do for your subsequent child is to take good care of yourself. If you are doing well in your grieving process then your child will be doing well too. I hope that this book will help you explain what happened regarding your baby to this precious child that you now have in your arms.

Cathy Blanford

Dedicated to my baby big sister, Colleen,
whom I never knew,
and to my parents who loved her.

There are three people who live at my house.

We have fun together.

We like to go to the park, and sometimes we stop to have ice cream on the way home.

There are three people who live at my house, but there are four people in my family.

Before I was born, Mommy and Daddy had another baby.

She was a girl baby and she died.

Sister

It may not always be comfortable to use such direct language with a child, but it is the clearest, least confusing way to explain to your child what happened to your baby. You might also use words such as "Our baby was born too soon." or "Our baby was too small (or too sick) to live." The more clear and simple explanation you are able to give, the more likely it is that your child will not worry about other important people in his life dying.

My Baby

Big Sister

Sometimes I feel mixed up about it because she was only a baby, but she was my big sister, too.

It can be confusing for a child to have the baby in pictures referred to as a "big sister," although if she had lived, she would indeed have been your child's big or older sibling. This will become clearer as you explain more to your child about what happened to your baby and as your child grows. It's good to give children information from the beginning in words that they can understand and to add to the story as they are more and more able to comprehend it.

My mommy and daddy were very sad when my baby big sister died.

They had been excited about having a baby coming to live with them.

There is no problem with your subsequent child knowing that you were sad when your baby died and that you are still sad at times when you think about what happened. This is an honest feeling and carefully sharing your true feelings is a good thing. It is also really important to make sure your child knows he's not responsible for making you feel better.

After my
baby big sister died,
Mommy and Daddy thought
about her for a long time.

They remembered her and
missed her very much.

Mommy and Daddy
would go to the cemetery
to visit the place
where she was buried.

They have a special box
that they keep on the shelf.

It has her pictures,
her clothes, and
her footprints in it.

They would look at these
things.

If you have such a box, your subsequent child will probably be curious about it. It is a good idea to share these things with your child if he is interested. You can choose a time that is good for you and take the opportunity to talk more about the baby with your subsequent child and to answer questions that arise.

Sometimes when they
saw other people
with babies,
or when they were out
walking and saw a beautiful
butterfly nearby,
they would think about her.

It could help your subsequent child to know some of the things
that stimulate memories of your baby. This will become one of
the ways that your child can be a part of the family's story.

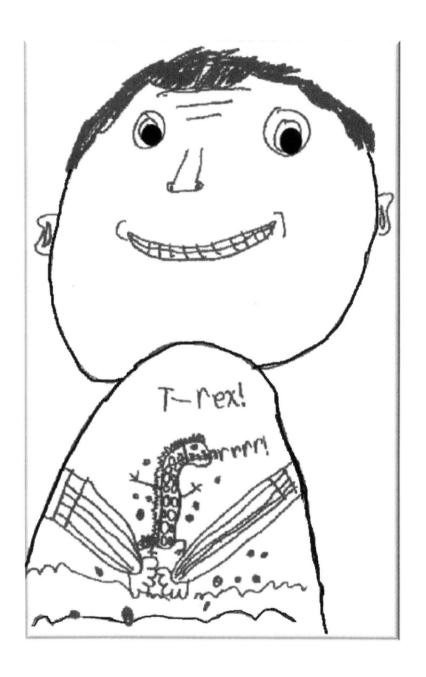

T-rex!

After some time
went by,
Mommy and Daddy decided
that they were ready to
love a new baby.

That's when they had me!

This is the best part of the story for your subsequent child—the place where he comes in!

Even though they remembered my baby big sister, when I was born, they loved holding me in their arms.

They loved rocking me and feeding me and showing me off to their friends.

They loved the color of my eyes and they loved the way that I smiled whenever I saw their faces.

Concrete examples of all of the things that you love about your subsequent child will help that child to truly understand and believe how special and wanted he is. No one will ever replace your baby who died, but this child who is with you now is a new and wonderful and different person, who needs to know that he is loved for himself.

Now that I am big,
Mommy and Daddy
talk to me
about my baby big sister.

Sometimes we go to the
cemetery together
to remember her.

Remembering your baby who died will always be a part of your family's story. Now that your subsequent child is a part of your family, it will be important to include him in this remembering even though your child has no memories of his own of the baby.

Our Baby ♡

Sometimes we look at the pictures and clothes and footprints together.

Sometimes I like to do these things, and sometimes I just feel like playing.

All of these activities are things that you can do to include your subsequent child. Sometimes your child will be curious about the baby and sometimes he won't and that is really normal.

Sometimes I see a
butterfly in the yard,
and I say to
Mommy and Daddy,
"Are you thinking about my
baby big sister?"

It's okay
for me to talk about it,
and I can ask questions
when I have them.

Be prepared for your subsequent child to bring up the subject of the baby when you least expect it. Your child is probably very attuned to your emotions and may be aware of when you are thinking about your baby. Knowing he can talk about it and ask questions is really good for him.

Sometimes I wonder
what it would have been like
if my baby big sister
did not die.

I wonder what it would have been like to have a big sister who lived at our house and could play with me.

I'll bet she would have loved going to the park and stopping for ice cream on the way home.

Big Sister

It is probably true that your subsequent child thinks about what it would have been like to have a big sister or brother who also lives at your house. While there may be some feelings of ambivalence, there is probably also a sense of wishing that it were true.

There are four people in my family and three people who live at my house.

Mommy, Daddy, and I love each other and have fun together, and we remember my baby big sister.

The repetition of this phrase "four people in my family and three people who live at my house" will be reassuring to your subsequent child as he works to understand and be a part of the life event that happened in your family before he was born. The most important thing is that your subsequent child always knows that he is loved for who he is.

Illustrations

MY BABY BIG SISTER was illustrated by Olivia (13) and Jackson (9) Paus, whose baby brother Eliot died, and by Reno (10) and Ally (8) Sarussi, grandchildren of the author. Their simple drawings depict a child's understanding of the events described in the book.

37877751R00025

Made in the USA
Lexington, KY
16 December 2014